AWESOME
ART
THAILAND

10 works from the land of the smiling
elephant that everyone should know

This book belongs to

by Clare Veal

Sawadee kha and welcome to Thailand! My name is Chang the elephant. I look very cute and am also pretty important. Elephants are the national emblem of Thailand, and I was even on the country's flag! I am so excited to guide you through the art of this diverse country.

Did you know that Thailand used to be called Siam? The country changed its name in 1939 to *"prathet Thai,"* which is sometimes translated as "Land of the Free."

Thailand is also the only country in Southeast Asia that was never colonised. Instead, the country has been ruled by the kings of the Chakri dynasty. They were in charge until 1932, when the country became a constitutional monarchy. This means that, even though the king remains the head of state, a government makes decisions. Through the years however, the monarchy has had a big impact on Thai art and culture as patrons, subjects for artworks, and even as artists!

Thailand's neighbours have also influenced its art and culture in different ways. The country is located right in the middle of mainland Southeast Asia, and shares borders with Cambodia, Laos, Malaysia, and Myanmar. Visitors from Europe, China, India, and elsewhere have also exchanged ideas with Thai artists, leading to new subjects and approaches in art making.

There are so many different ideas about what Thai art can be and so many creative artists to learn about. Come with me and let's explore them together!

ROYAL CHILDREN WITH CAMERAS (EARLY 20TH CENTURY)

BY AN UNKNOWN PHOTOGRAPHER

Today, taking a photograph is as simple as touching a button. But in the early 20th century, producing photographs was not that easy. Cameras were expensive, and photography required special equipment and training which were not available to most people.

However, for the Siamese elite who could afford it, photography was a fun pastime. King Chulalongkorn, the fifth monarch of the Chakri dynasty, loved to take photographs during his travels. He also asked foreign photographers in Bangkok, like Emil Groote from Germany, for their advice on different photographic methods to improve his technique.

Other members of King Chulalongkorn's family, including his wives and children, also caught the photography "bug." They enjoyed playing with cameras and taking photographs of each other around the Palace, like in this photograph, or in specially-constructed sets. Some photographs even show them in funny poses or fancy dress!

PHOTOGRAPHING THE KING

Unlike Europe, where there had been a tradition of portraiture before photography was invented, in Siam, artists were actually forbidden to make images of the king because it was believed he was too powerful to look at. This all changed in 1845 when a French priest named Father Larnaudie brought the first daguerreotype camera to Bangkok. Ten years later, King Mongkut sat for a daguerreotype portrait, which is believed to be the first public image of a Thai king.

Why do you think the King decided to have his photograph taken? We know from historical archives that his first photograph was sent as a gift to England's Queen Victoria, along with a letter in which the King called her his "sister." In the following years, the King also sent photographs to other leaders including the Pope, Emperor Napoleon III of France, and the United States' then-President Franklin Pierce. This was the King's way of developing friendships between Siam and other nations.

CHECK OUT THIS PIN—HOLE CAMERA! LEARN HOW TO MAKE YOUR OWN ON P 10 AND 11.

EARLY PHOTOGRAPHY

Try sitting perfectly still for five minutes without moving. It's tricky, isn't it? The daguerreotype, invented by Louise Daguerre in France in 1839, is thought to be the world's first photographic process, and sometimes required portrait sitters to stay still for more than an hour!

Making a daguerreotype was a very technical process that involved dangerous chemicals like mercury, cyanide, and sulfuric acid. Unlike photographs from later techniques, daguerreotypes could not be reproduced. These photographs were thus very precious, so people would store them away safely in ornate cases.

MAKE YOUR OWN PINHOLE CAMERA!

A pinhole camera works by allowing light to shine into the box from a single opening, called an aperture. When light shines through the aperture, it produces an inverted image of an outside scene in the camera. This effect is known as the *camera obscura* effect.

Create your own pinhole camera! You will need an empty shoebox with a lid, a sharp pencil, a pair of scissors, a ruler, wax paper, tape, a blanket, and a penknife. Be careful with the penknife or ask an adult for help with it!

Step 1: With the point of the pencil, punch a hole in the center of one of the shorter ends of the shoebox.

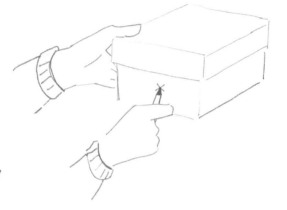

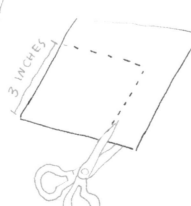

Step 2: Using the penknife, cut out a 5 x 5cm square in the opposite end of the shoebox, across from the hole from step 1.

Step 3: Cut a square of wax paper to cover the square. This should measure about 7 x 7 cm on each side.

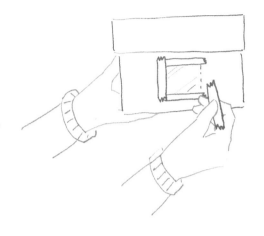

Step 4: Tape the wax paper over the square. You now have a pinhole camera!

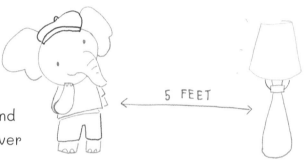

Step 5: Find a dark room and switch on a single lamp. Cover your head and the pinhole camera with a blanket, ensuring that the end with the aperture is pointed at the lamp and not covered by the blanket.

5 FEET

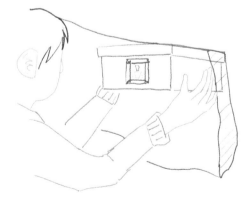

Step 6: Hold your pinhole camera at arms-length from your face. You should see an upside-down image of the lamp appear on the wax paper square!

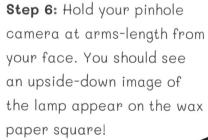

HER MAJESTY QUEEN SRI BAJARINDRA OF SIAM (C.1896)

BY ROBERT LENZ

Does this photograph of Queen Sri Bajarindra remind you of any other works of art? In the 19th century, studio photographers drew from European oil portraits to flatter their wealthy clients. When we look at the Queen, we are meant to be impressed by the expensive objects around her. She is also photographed with a painted backdrop that makes it seem like she is in a palace.

During the colonial period, foreign photographers set up studios all over Southeast Asia. The German photographer Robert Lenz opened his first studio in Rangoon, Burma (now known as Myanmar) in 1892. Four years later he launched a second branch in Singapore, where he took this photograph of the Queen, as well as several others of her husband King Chulalongkorn and their children. The King liked the photographs so much, he later invited Lenz to become his official photographer in Bangkok!

WOW, SHE LOOKS SO REGAL! WHAT OBJECTS WOULD YOU CHOOSE FOR YOUR OWN PORTRAIT? WRITE THEM DOWN ON P 14!

เสาวภาผ่องศรี

Sowabah Pongsri

Robert Lenz & Co
PHOTOGRAPHERS

SINGAPORE
CORNER OF STAMFORD ROAD & HILL St.

11

SIWILAI

In Siam, European trends were called "*siwilai*," which is the Thai way of saying "civilized." *Siwilai* could include everything from music to architecture, and even eating with a knife and fork! Even though these trends came from Europe, they were usually adjusted to suit local tastes. For instance, while elite Siamese women liked to wear European-style blouses with big, puffy sleeves (known as "leg o'mutton"), they would also usually style these with short trousers made from Thai silk, called *jong kraben*.

By adopting European fashions and behaviours, the Siamese elite hoped to show that they were as "civilized" as their European counterparts, to establish their position as a "leader" in the region. However, they also wanted to counter the flimsy excuse given by European powers for colonisation: that it was necessary because certain areas of the world were "undeveloped."

THE KING'S WIVES

King Chulalongkorn had 92 wives and more than 77 children! They lived in a special area of the royal compound known as the Inner Palace. The Inner Palace was like a mini city, and because no other adult men (apart from the King) were allowed to enter, the women inhabitants ran it by themselves!

By taking on administrative roles or giving birth to royal children, the King's wives could also increase their own status. This was the case with Queen Sri Bajarindra. She was the King's most important wife because as his half-sister, she also had royal blood, and she had given birth to a son who became Crown Prince in 1895. Two years later she became Siam's first woman regent and, in 1904, she established her own school for girls!

Dusit Palace, the residence of King Chulalongkorn

REGENT FOR A DAY!

Imagine you were selecting props for your very own studio portrait. Create a checklist of these items in the space below.

What objects would you choose to display around you?

What clothes would you wear to show off today's fashions?

How would you pose in your studio portrait?

FACE (1956)

BY FUA HARIBHITAK

What catches your eye when you look at this painting? Although the work's geometric shapes look random, they are actually thoughtfully arranged in what we call a composition. If you look carefully, you will see diagonal lines pointing towards the center of the work, as well as curved forms that draw our eyes to the face.

The artist of this work, Fua Haribhitak, loved to experiment with different styles of painting. When he was studying at Poh Chang art school in the 1930s, his adventurous attitude got him into trouble, and he even failed one of his final exams! When he became a professional artist, he made mural paintings for Buddhist temples, while also painting portraits in an impressionistic style, with dark colours and visible brushstrokes.

OOHH~

I SEE TWO EYES, A NOSE AND A MOUTH.

CUBISM IN THAILAND AND BEYOND

Face shows Fua's interest in Cubism, a movement he was introduced to while studying in Italy from 1954 to 1956. Once he returned to Thailand, he shared the books and artworks he had bought overseas with his friends and colleagues. As a result, many of them became interested in European modern art too! By the late 1950s and 1960s, Cubism had become a very popular art style in Thailand.

However, not everyone in the Thai art world was so enthusiastic. In fact, some critics warned that Thai artists should be careful when experimenting with styles and techniques like Cubism in order to avoid losing their Thai identity.

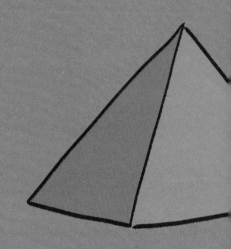

IS THERE 'RIGHT' OR 'WRONG' WHEN IT COMES TO MAKING ART? WHY DO YOU SAY SO?

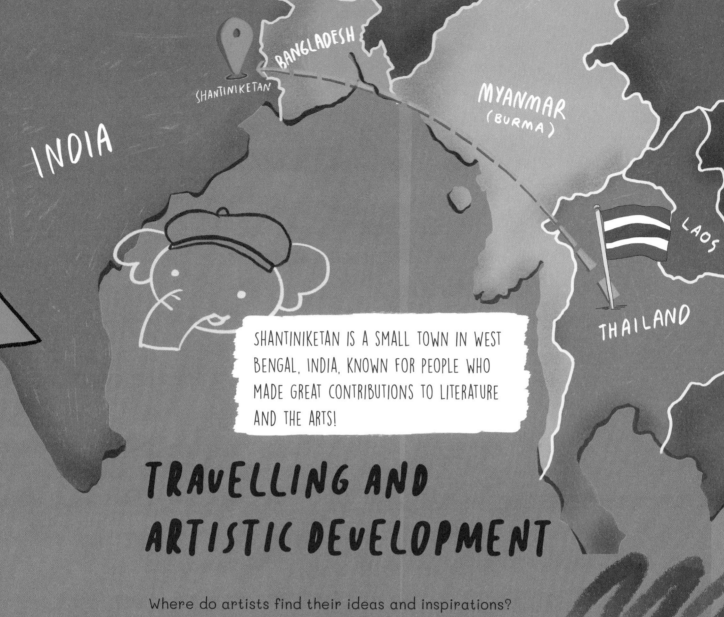

SHANTINIKETAN IS A SMALL TOWN IN WEST BENGAL, INDIA, KNOWN FOR PEOPLE WHO MADE GREAT CONTRIBUTIONS TO LITERATURE AND THE ARTS!

TRAVELLING AND ARTISTIC DEVELOPMENT

Where do artists find their ideas and inspirations? Some, like Fua, developed completely new approaches after travelling to new places.

Before travelling to Italy, Fua left Thailand in 1941 to study at Kala Bhavana, an important art school established in Shantiniketan, India by the Nobel Prize winning poet, Rabindarinath Tagore. Many artists from across Asia studied there and learnt from each other, including Bagyi Aung Soe from Myanmar and Affandi from Indonesia. This not only helped them develop new directions in their work, it also helped them reimagine what modern Asian art could be!

WHAT IS CUBISM?

Cubism was an art movement that was developed by artists like Pablo Picasso and Georges Braque in Europe in the early 1900s. It was part of a broader group of art movements that forms what we call Modernism.

Prior to Modernism, European artists had been interested in making paintings look like they were windows onto other worlds. Although they were paintings, these works were meant to look almost like the real thing. But by the end of the 19th century, painters became less interested in representing the world "objectively," as a photograph might, and started to think about how people "really" see.

To better understand how to "see" like a Cubist artist, try sitting in front of an object and thinking carefully about the movement of your eyes as you observe it. Do your eyes stay completely still, or do they roam around the object and its surroundings?

Cubism developed this idea by representing, in a single painting, how we observe an object over time. They did this by painting things from multiple points of view and reducing them to basic shapes.

Picasso was influenced by African art, which was seen as shocking to European audiences at the time. Artists outside of Europe interpreted Cubism in many different ways. For example, art historian Partha Mitter has suggested that in India, Cubism was a way to critique colonialism.

WHAT DO YOU THINK CUBISM COULD MEAN IN SOUTHEAST ASIA?

MOTHER (1961)

BY SOMPOT UPA-IN

Sculpture is a very important medium in Thailand because it is commonly used to represent the figure of the Buddha. From the mid-19th century, Thai kings also asked artists to make sculptural portraits of them and other important people to display in public places.

Sompot Upa-In's work *Mother* is different from these other sculptures, because the people he represents are not supposed to be identified. Instead, the artist chose to simplify these forms by ignoring details like fingers and strands of hair. This style is called semi-abstraction—even though we can tell that the sculpture is of two people, their appearance is stylized into basic shapes, abstractions of human figures.

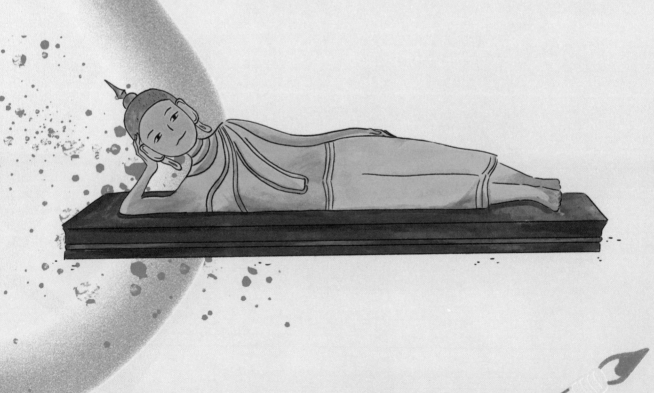

SILPA BHIRASRI AND SILPAKORN UNIVERSITY

Sompot learned a lot about sculpture from his teacher Corrado Feroci, an Italian artist who moved to Thailand in 1923 to teach "Western Sculpture" at the Fine Arts Department of the Ministry of Palace Affairs. In Thailand, he produced many monuments of historical figures, a subject matter not found in traditional Thai sculpture. Feroci liked Thailand so much that he decided to become a citizen, and changed his name to Silpa Bhirasri.

Bhirasri is now known as the father of Thai modern art because he founded the country's first "modern" art school, Silpakorn University, in 1933. Several artists in this book, as well as many figures in Thailand's art world, attended this school. One of Bhirasri's key ideas was that Thai artists should show their national character in their artworks, even when taking influence from elsewhere. As you read the rest of this book, think about how much influence Bhirasri's ideas had, and if there are Thai artists who don't fit this mould.

Silpakorn University

WHAT DO YOU THINK "NATIONAL CHARACTER" IS? WHAT MIGHT BE THE NATIONAL CHARACTER OF THE ART WHERE YOU'RE FROM?

THE NATIONAL ART EXHIBITION

How do we know what good art is? Bhirasri set up the National Art Exhibition in 1949, and it became one of the most important ways for artists to gain recognition. But not everyone agrees on what types of art should be celebrated.

Silpakorn students and staff always seemed to win the National Exhibition awards, which displeased some artists including Sompot. Sompot and his friends also didn't like that the National Exhibition had rules that limited the types of works that could be shown to paintings, prints and sculptures. So, in 1979, Sompot and his friends formed the Artist's Society of Thailand. The group organised exhibitions which allowed works of any medium, by artists of any age, to be shown!

EVERYDAY SCULPTURE

Assemble your own abstract sculpture with materials you can find around the house!

Look around the house and let your imagination run free—you might see simple geometric shapes in objects like toilet rolls, jars or containers. Put them together to form a human figure!

What else can you find? Can you reassemble your chosen objects into other forms, like an animal?

TOILET ROLLS

CARDBOARD

NOTEBOOK

JARS

BALL

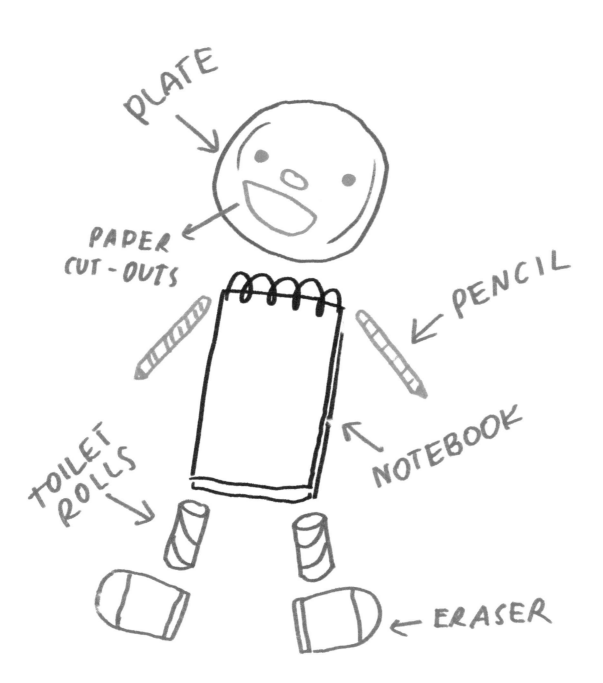

PLATE

PAPER
CUT-OUTS

PENCIL

NOTEBOOK

TOILET
ROLLS

ERASER

THE ORCHARDMAN'S SMILE (1976)

BY PRATUANG EMJAROEN

Sometimes artistic inspiration can be found in the things we see every day. The artist who painted this work, Pratuang Emjaroen, came up with many of his ideas while walking and meditating in the rice fields and forests of the Thai countryside. He was so in love with nature that he tried to capture this sensory experience in his art. The bright colours he used in this painting really brings out the heat of Thailand's tropical climate!

MY STOMACH IS RUMBLING! IT MUST BE BECAUSE OF ALL THE DELICIOUS LOOKING FRUITS AND VEGETABLES IN THIS PAINTING! HOW MANY DIFFERENT KINDS CAN YOU SPOT? WHAT DO YOU THINK THEY SMELL AND TASTE LIKE?

STUDENT BECOMES MASTER

Although some artists, like Sompot on p 22, learn to be artists by going to art schools such as Silpakorn University, others, like Pratuang, teach themselves!

Pratuang came from a poor family and left school when he was only ten years old to support them. As a teenager, one of his jobs was painting cinema billboards, which developed his interest in art and culture. He finally decided to become a full-time artist, but didn't have the same opportunities as the artists who studied at Silpakorn. He developed his career and eventually achieved success by learning from and exhibiting with other self-taught artists.

WOW! PRATUANG WOULD HAVE PAINTED A CINEMA BILLBOARD JUST LIKE THIS!

Pratuang Emjaroen

STRONGER TOGETHER

The 1970s were a tumultuous time in Thailand. The country was under a military dictatorship, and a war was being fought between the United States and several countries on Thailand's doorstep, including Laos, Cambodia, and Vietnam. During this period, the US even used Thailand to host several military bases!

In this context, many Thai students and workers decided to protest against the US presence in their country, as well as their government's unfair policies, like letting companies from overseas not pay taxes in Thailand. Young artists like Pratuang, who became involved in these politics, believed that art was not just something nice to look at, but a tool to make society better for everyone. They also knew that they could never achieve these goals as individuals, so they organised themselves into collectives like the Artists Front of Thailand or the Dhamma Group, to develop strength in numbers.

ARTISTS IN SOLIDARITY!

We can support causes we believe in by expressing our solidarity with those affected, and making art is an effective way to do so. Whether the cause you champion is climate change, human rights or animal welfare, it can be portrayed in the form of a poster. Sketch a draft of your poster in the space below!

CITIES ON THE MOVE 6 (1999)

BY NAVIN RAWANCHAIKUL AND RIRKRIT TIRAVANIJA

The bold colours and letters in this painting by Navin Rawanchaikul and Rirkrit Tiravanija make it look like a movie poster, the kind you might see promoting a film. Can you imagine what this film would be about? The central figure, with his popped collar and weapon in each hand, could be the protagonist of an action film! The background also features cityscapes from Thailand and Austria, so maybe this adventure takes place all around the world—the title of the exhibition in which it was shown, *Cities on the Move*, certainly implies this.

In contrast to their modernist counterparts, Thai contemporary artists, like Rirkrit and Navin, often use everyday materials and subject matter to explore the relationship between art and life. Navin's artworks borrow from popular culture, including cinema, advertising, and comic books. Using these forms, he often portrays his friends and family as different characters in situations he imagines.

Rirkrit, on the other hand, likes to use art to help people meet and socialise. He is perhaps best known for his artwork *untitled (free/still)* (1992/1995/2007), in which he cooked and served Thai vegetable curry to people in a gallery. People sat around the space, enjoying the delicious food with one another.

ตุ๊กตุ๊กภาพยนตร์ ภูมิใจเสนอ
ตค-2542
กรุงเทพมหานคร
ทะลุมิติสู่กรุงเทพฯ แห่งอนาคต
CITIES ON THE MOVE 6
นำโดย
โฆษิต / อ้อม / อาริน / ฟองซีน
ลักขณา / เหมียว / เจี๊ยบ / โก๋ / โดมินิค
และเพื่อนพ้องอีกมากมาย
เมืองบ้าบา 6
5 รางวัลตุ๊กตาทอง เป็นหลักประกัน
* ผลงานของ 2 ผู้กำกับมือทอง
เสี่ยวิน และ เฮียฤทธิ์ รับประกันความบันเทิง
ดาวร้าย!
ฮันส์ / ฮันรู
โทมัส / โอเล่
ไมเคิล

BEYOND THE GALLERY

Does an artwork have to be shown in a gallery for us to call it "art"? For their *Cities on the Move* project, Navin and Rirkrit wanted to surprise audiences by displaying their art where people would least expect it. As part of this work, the artists decorated three-wheeled *tuk tuks* that drove around the streets of Vienna, Austria! While *tuk tuks* are a common sight in Thailand, what do you think passers-by thought when they saw one driving in Austria?

WHILE IT MIGHT SEEM CONFUSING THAT THIS WORK IS CONSIDERED ART, IN FACT, IT MAKES US QUESTION HOW WE DEFINE ART AND WHAT AN ARTIST DOES.

WHAT MAKES A THAI ARTIST?

When we write a history of Thai art, what works should we include? Do these works have to express a Thai "national character," as Bhirasri thought on p 24, or do the artists have to live in Thailand? Navin and Rirkrit's personal histories show us that Thai art is not limited to experiences within the country itself!

Navin's family moved from Pakistan to Thailand before he was born, during a difficult period in Pakistan's history. His work often explores his family's history of migration and the experiences of the migrant community in Thailand.

Rirkrit, on the other hand, was born to Thai parents in Argentina and moved all over the world as a child. He now he spends his time between the US, Germany, and Thailand. His experience of travel has also influenced his work, and he loves to produce imaginative maps and diagrams of his movements!

ABOUT YOU

Imagine you're making a new friend. What are some
things about yourself that you would want them to know?

Think about your favourite colours, films you've seen,
the places you've been, and the people close to you.

On the next page, introduce yourself by creating an
online profile. You can draw a portrait of yourself, and
fill in the blanks with your favourite things!

CHANG

ABOUT ME!
- FAVE COLOR : ORANGE
- A FILM I LOVE : HORTON HEARS A WHO! (2008)
- I LOVE IT WHEN MY
  FRIENDS AND I APPRECIATE
  ART TOGETHER ♥

TODAY!
↳ I'M FEELING .... CURIOUS 00?

ABOUT ME!

- FAVORITE COLOR:
- A FILM I LOVE:
- MY FAVORITE ARTWORK IN THIS BOOK:

- I LOVE WHEN MY FRIENDS AND I..:

DRAW YOUR ICON!

(YOUR USERNAME)

TODAY!

↳ I'M FEELING....

When you're actually online, be aware of who you're sharing your information with. And when in doubt, always ask an adult.

SHOCKING PINK COLLECTION (1998)

BY MANIT SRIWANICHPOOM

Check out that man in pink! His exaggerated poses make him look quite absurd, and his shiny pink clothes make him look so out of place! He's dressed so loudly and garishly; you would spot him from a mile away. In fact, this funny man isn't a real person, but a character called The Pink Man created by artist Manit Sriwanichpoom. But why is he pink?

A good place to start hunting for clues about the meaning of this work is its caption, which you can find on p 63. These are, in fact, digital photographs which have been presented as lightboxes. You might find lightboxes like these at bus stops or on buildings, usually for advertisements as they attract a lot of attention!

Next, let's take a look at the year that the artwork was made in. What was happening around 1998 that might have motivated Manit to produce this work? In 1997, the Asian Financial Crisis began in Thailand. Many people lost their jobs, poverty became more widespread, and inequality worsened. For artists like Manit, the excessive advertisements that encouraged people to buy more things did not make any sense when people were suffering.

Now let's piece together this information. It seems to me that the work's date and medium link the Pink Man to ideas about advertising and consumerism. Look closely at the images. Do you think this character is the artist's way of telling us to buy lots of things? Or is he warning us about what might happen if we only care about money and material things?

THE ROLE OF THE ARTIST

What do you think is the role of an artist? Do they make beautiful pictures for people to appreciate or provide different perspectives through their art, new ways of looking at the world?

According to Manit, an artist's role is political because he or she can give voice to different perspectives on important issues. In this way, his ideas are quite similar to the artist collectives from the 1970s on p 31, who believed art can help ordinary people!

Manit also works with other artists to achieve his goals. For instance, in the same year he created *Shocking Pink Collection*, he worked with other artists to produce an installation to support villagers from Phrae in northern Thailand, who were protesting a dam project that would have damaged the local environment. The installation drew upon the local knowledge of the village by using materials and symbols that were familiar to its inhabitants.

NATIONALISM

Wherever we grow up, we are usually taught to respect our country. This bond between people who live in the same place and share some of the same values is called "nationalism."

However, sometimes citizens will disagree about what beliefs should be promoted, and some will critique the dominant form of nationalism. This can be seen in *Shocking Pink Collection*, where Manit has photographed his friend, Sompong Tawee, dressing up as different "Thai" stereotypes that reflect some of the ways these national values are interpreted. Sompong's poses and dress make it difficult to take these roles seriously, making us realise how silly they can be!

CONSUME, CONSUME, CONSUME!

Through the Pink Man, Manit shows us how absurd it is for big companies to promote their goods and encourage people to buy things they may not actually need. Look closely at the photographs from p 40 to 44. The Pink Man is posing in a different place, doing something different, in each one.

From the photographs, what do you think the Pink Man has bought? Circle the correct answers below!

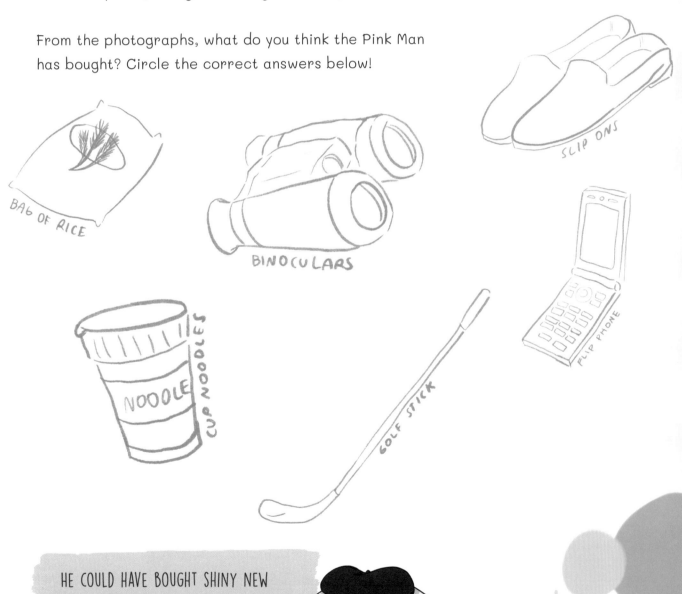

BAG OF RICE

BINOCULARS

SLIP ONS

CUP NOODLES

NOOOLE

GOLF STICK

FLIP PHONE

HE COULD HAVE BOUGHT SHINY NEW OBJECTS, BUT WHAT ABOUT TRIPS ABROAD? DOES THAT COUNT AS CONSUMPTION TOO?

SITTING (2004)

BY KAMIN LERTCHAIPRASERT

Although Kamin Lertchaiprasert's *Sitting* is made up of small sculptures, it can take up a whole room in the gallery! The artist produced one of these wooden figures every day for an entire leap year. That makes 366 sculptures in total!

Looking at this work on display in a gallery, we first notice that all of the figures are a similar size and all of them appear to be in a seated position. But on closer inspection, we see that each figure is different. Some have big smiles, some have multiple arms, and others have flowers coming out of their heads!

WHICH OF THESE SCULPTURES IS YOUR FAVOURITE? CAN YOU COME UP WITH A DIFFERENT POSE?

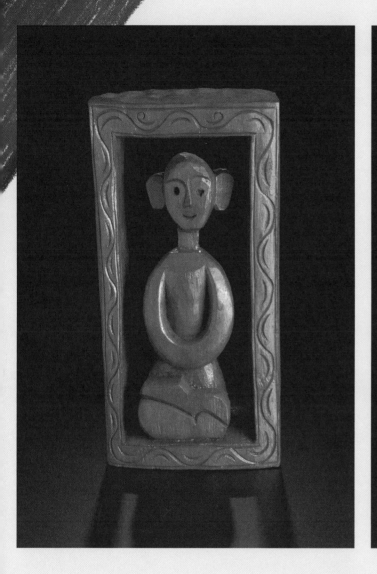

ART IN MEDITATION

Kamin made one figure every day to practice and reflect his belief that art-making is meditative. Meditation is the practice of emptying the mind of thoughts and focusing on the present; here, Kamin focused on creating a sculpture. The artist's dedication to making something every day links back to some of the core ideas in Theravada Buddhism, including the belief that time is just a series of passing moments.

Buddhist stories and characters have been an important subject in Thai art since premodern times, and contemporary artists like Kamin have found new ways to explore Buddhism in their art.

THERAVADA IS THE OLDEST EXISTING SCHOOL OF BUDDHISM! IT IS THE FORM OF BUDDHISM MOST WIDELY PRACTISED IN THAILAND.

Wat Benchamabophit (Marble Temple)

48

CHIANG MAI AS AN ART CITY

For a long time, Bangkok was the center of Thailand's art world. This was because it is home to Silpakorn University, as well as many galleries and museums. This changed in the 1980s when a faculty of fine arts opened at Chiang Mai University in northern Thailand, and several important artists moved there to become teachers. This developed an art community in the city that Kamin is now a part of.

Because Chiang Mai did not have many galleries, the artists who lived there had to come up with new ways to exhibit their works. In 1992, a group of artists living in the city got together to organise a festival called Chiang Mai Social Installation, which used the whole city as a gallery! This event attracted artists from all over the world, who displayed their art and did performances in all sorts of unexpected places, including libraries and temples. This spirit of experimentation still exists in Chiang Mai, and in Kamin's practice too!

A CIRCLE A DAY

There are seven circles in the space below. Every day this week, draw an image in the circle—it can be of whatever comes to mind!

Pay careful attention to what you draw, and how your drawings change through the week. While making these drawings, you might take some time to think about the events of your day and how you feel in the moment.

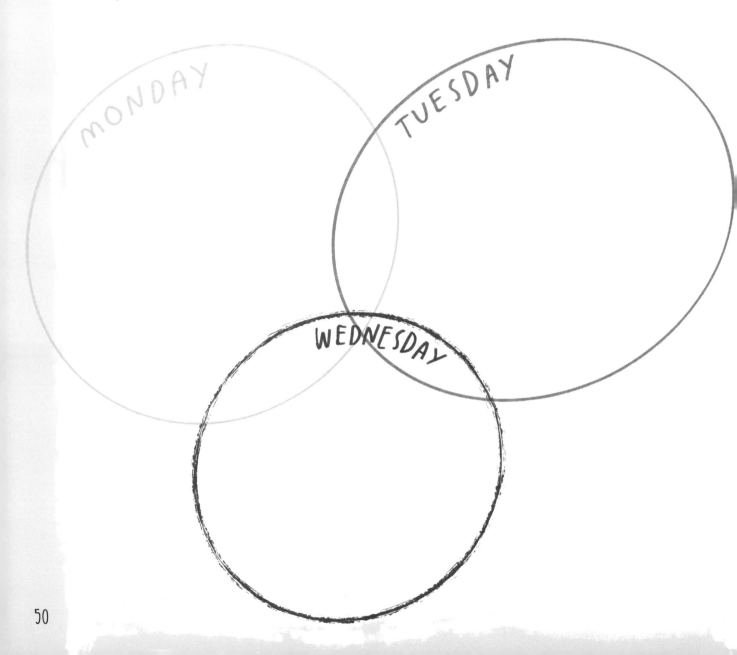

SATURDAY

FRIDAY

SUNDAY

THURSDAY

NOON-NOM (2001-2003)

BY PINAREE SANPITAK

We often only think about art in terms of what we can see. But our other senses are as important to the experience of art! In this work by Pinaree Sanpitak, we are encouraged to play amongst huge pink, grey, white, and black cushions. This work is designed to be touched, so the artist had to think about how these cushions would feel against the audience's skin. This is why she used multiple types of fabric to produce different sensations.

While the feel of the cushions is important, their shape is also very interesting. Pinaree is known for making artworks in the shape of breasts. She was inspired to use this shape after she gave birth and began breastfeeding her son. Since then, she has used different materials to explore this form, from hard steel structures you can walk around, to piles of rice you can eat! Because her breast works come in different sizes, they can also resemble other objects, like the stupas of Thai Buddhist temples.

INSTALLATION ART IN THAILAND

What is the difference between sculpture and installation? Even though they are both three-dimensional art forms, installation often engages multiple senses, and usually interacts with the space in which it is displayed.

Installation art became popular in Thailand in the 1990s, with artists using local, everyday materials including silk, herbs, ceramics, and straw to explore their own identities. In this way, Thai artists like Pinaree and Araya Rasdjarmrearnsook, whose work we'll see on p 58, were similar to other Southeast Asian artists working at the same time. In fact, some art historians have argued that installation is a Southeast Asian medium because of its similarities to local craft and ceremonial traditions.

IF YOU WANT TO BECOME AN ART HISTORIAN, YOU COULD THINK ABOUT RESEARCHING WOMEN ARTISTS!

WOMANIFESTO

You might have noticed that in art history books women artists are not mentioned as often as male artists. This is because women are not always given the same opportunities as men. Art historians are working hard to find and write about more women artists, but there is still a lot of work to be done!

Womanifesto is one important project that addresses this issue, by giving women opportunities to exhibit their work, make art, and connect with one another. Its name, "Womanifesto," is a combination of two words: "woman" and "manifesto." It was set up in 1997 by a group of artists including Varsha Nair, Nitaya Ueareeworakul, and Phaptawan Suwannakudt. Its activities have attracted artists from all over the world!

REMEMBER THE NAME

Can you remember the names of the notable artists and projects mentioned in this book so far? Test your knowledge by filling in this crossword puzzle! Use the clues provided to help you. Find the answers on p 57!

1. Siam's first woman regent.

2. An artist who used different types of fabric in her installation.

3. The photographer who captured a portrait of Siam's first woman regent.

4. An important project that gave women the opportunity to exhibit their work, make art, and network.

5. A woman artist who was part of Womananifesto, who also works with installations and is featured in this book!

TWO PLANETS (2007-2008)

BY ARAYA RASDJARMREARNSOOK

In Araya Rasdjarmreansook's video work, *Two Planets*, a group of Thai villagers look at and discuss famous paintings by European artists like Pierre-Auguste Renoir and Édouard Manet. These artworks are familiar to Western audiences, who tend to share similar ideas about what they mean. But for the Thai villagers, they are completely new! It is so interesting for us to learn about their perspectives and how they understand these paintings in relation to their lives in northern Thailand.

VIDEO ART OR FILM?

Now that museums show lots of screen-based art, it can be difficult to tell whether something is a video art piece or a film. And when artists, work across both mediums, it becomes even more complicated!

While there is no easy way to determine whether something is a film or a video work, we can start by looking at its content. Films often have a narrative and characters, while video art tends to be more experimental. Video artists like Araya also often think more carefully about how their work is displayed, perhaps using multiple screens or different types of seating for the audience, like old, wooden chairs. But even with these clues, some works are still too difficult to categorize, so scholars simply use the term "moving image" to describe them instead.

WHO DECIDES ON WHAT AN ARTWORK MEANS? WHEN TWO PEOPLE LOOK AT THE SAME WORK, DO THEY UNDERSTAND IT IN THE SAME WAY? WHAT ABOUT WHEN THEY ARE FROM DIFFERENT CULTURES OR BACKGROUNDS?

THAI ART ON THE INTERNATIONAL STAGE

"BIENNALE" IS ITALIAN FOR "BIENNIAL" MEANING "EVERY OTHER YEAR." IT IS COMMONLY USED IN THE ART WORLD TO DESCRIBE LARGE INTERNATIONAL CONTEMPORARY ART EXHIBITIONS THAT HAPPEN EVERY OTHER YEAR.

Like many contemporary Thai artists, Araya has participated in biennales in cities all over the world. And the title *Two Planets* refers to the different worlds she inhabits: a rural community in Chiang Mai and the international art world.

But Thai artists have not always been so internationally visible. In fact, in the 1990s curators like Apinan Poshyananda had to work hard to promote Thai artists overseas. For instance, in 1996 Apinan opened the exhibition *Contemporary Art in Asia: Traditions/Tensions* at the Asia Society in New York City. While some audiences appreciated being exposed to new types of contemporary art from South and Southeast Asia, others were confused because the works did not conform to their expectations of what "Asian" art is.

SAME PLANET?

Select an artwork from this book and look at it with a friend or family member. Discuss what the artwork reminds you of. You could think about:

The artwork's subject matter: does it look like a person, or is it primarily a shape?

The meaning the artist is trying to convey.

The artwork's medium: is it a photograph, a painting, or a sculpture?

Are your interpretations the same or different?

ONE LAST LOOK

We've had such an amazing journey through the art of Thailand! The photographs, paintings, sculptures, and installations have given us so much to think about. Keep pondering these questions as you take one last look at the art we've seen!

Do visit National Gallery Singapore to see some of these artworks on display, or discover other awesome Thai artists. See you there soon!

Unknown photographer
Royal Children with Cameras

Early 20th century
Albumen print
23.0 x 29.0cm
Collection of Mr & Mrs Lee Kip Lee

Robert Lenz
Her Majesty Queen Sri Bajarindra of Siam

c. 1896
Silver gelatin print on paper
24.0 x 18.2 cm
Courtesy of the National Museum of Singapore, National Heritage Board

Sompot Upa-In
Mother

1961
Bronze
64.0 x 35.0 x 30.0 cm
© Isr Upa-in

Pratuang Emjaroen
The Orchardman's Smile

1976
Oil on canvas
154.0 x 135.8 cm

Fua Haribhitak
Face

c. 1956
Oil on canvas
65.0 x 55.0 cm

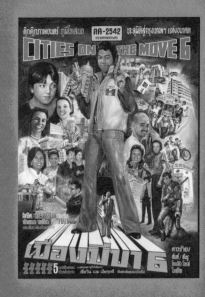

Navin
Rawanchaikul and
Rirkrit Tiravanija
*Cities on the Move
6, Bangkok*

1999
Acrylic on canvas,
170.0 x 120.0 cm
© Navin
Rawanchaikul and
Rirkrit Tiravanija

Manit
Sriwanichpoom
*Shocking Pink
Collection*

1998
Digital
photographs
150.0 x 100.0 cm
each

Kamin
Lertchaiprasert
Sitting

2004
Wood and wire
Collection of
Singapore Art
Museum

Pinaree Sanpitak
Noon-Nom

2011
Organza and
synthetic fiber
Collection of
Singapore Art
Museum

Araya
Rasdjarmrearnsook
Two Planets

2008
4-channel video, stereo,
720 x 576, 25fps, 48 kHz
Collection of
Singapore Art Museum

Published 2021

Please direct all enquiries to the publisher at:
National Gallery Singapore
1 St. Andrew's Road, #01-01 Singapore 178957

Author: Clare Veal
Managing Editor: Elaine Ee
Project Editors: Joyce Choong
Designer: Do Not Design
Illustrator: Sweet Gamboa

With kind assistance from:
Cheng Jia Yun, Debbi Tan, and Tiara Izzanty

National Library Board, Singapore Cataloguing in Publication Data
Name(s): Veal, Clare.
Title: Awesome art Thailand: 10 works from the land of the smiling elephant that everyone should know / Clare Veal.
Other title(s): Awesome art.
Description: Singapore: National Gallery Singapore, 2021.
Identifier(s): OCN 1200736787 - ISBN 978-981-14-8425-4 (paperback)
Subjects: LCSH: Art, Thai--Juvenile literature. | Art, Thai--Appreciation--Juvenile literature. | Art appreciation--Juvenile literature.
Classification: DDC 709.593--dc23